ESSENTIAL COMPUTERS

# INTERNET

# PARENTAL CONTROL

JAN HOWELLS & JOHN WATSON

A Dorling Kindersley Book

**Dorling Kindersley**
LONDON, NEW YORK, SYDNEY, DELHI,
PARIS, MUNICH, and JOHANNESBURG

Produced for Dorling Kindersley Limited by
Design Revolution, Queens Park Villa,
30 West Drive, Brighton, East Sussex BN2 2GE

EDITORIAL DIRECTOR Ian Whitelaw
SENIOR DESIGNER Andy Ashdown
PROJECT EDITOR John Watson
DESIGNER Paul Bowler

SENIOR EDITOR Mary Lindsay
SENIOR MANAGING ART EDITOR Nigel Duffield
DTP DESIGNER Jason Little
PRODUCTION CONTROLLER Michelle Thomas

Published in Great Britain in 2000 by
Dorling Kindersley Limited,
9 Henrietta Street, London WC2E 8PS

2 4 6 8 10 9 7 5 3 1

A CIP catalog record for this book is available from the British Library.

ISBN 0-7513-1298-3

Color reproduced by First Impressions, London
Printed in Italy by Graphicom

For our complete
catalog visit
**www.dk.com**

# CONTENTS

# WHAT IS THE INTERNET?

**On the simplest level, the internet is a communications network with traffic moving across it, just like older networks such as the railroad, the telephone, and radio communications.**

## UNDERSTANDING THE INTERNET

In the case of the internet, the network consists of telecommunications links connecting millions of computers. The links vary in their data-transmitting speed, and the computers vary immensely in their size, power, and content.

### THE ORIGINS OF THE INTERNET

The internet is the result of many different technologies being brought together. By the 1960s, once the rules for transmitting data between computers had been worked out, a "galactic network" of computers came under consideration. In 1969, four computers were linked together in California and Utah to form the first computer network, known as ARPANET, which grew during the 1970s. At the start of the 1980s, academic networks in the US and UK solved incompatibility problems, which allowed commercial networks to be added to the network. By the end of the 1980s, faster connections allowed the commercialization of the internet to expand.

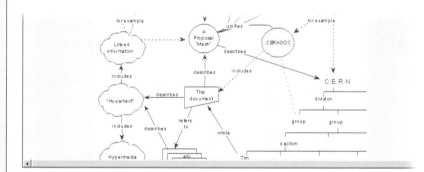

## THE BIRTH OF
## THE WORLD WIDE WEB

In 1989, a scientist named Tim Berners-Lee proposed a global project in which the existing internet network was used to store a web of interlinked documents stored on large computers called servers. Users accessed this web by using a piece of software called a *browser*, which would look for a link's address and then use rules (or *protocols*) to obtain the document. The protocol used was the HyperText Transfer Protocol (HTTP) to retrieve the document, which itself is coded in HTML (HyperText Markup Language). HTML tells the browser how to format and display the document onscreen. In the mid-1990s, the world wide web was made a separate entity within the internet, which stimulated global access, as well as developing the organization, and content, which could now be added to and accessed by anyone with a computer and a phone line.

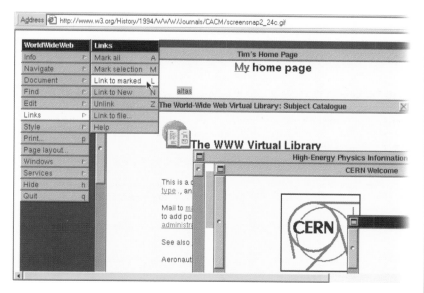

*(Above) This is a web browser developed by Tim Berners-Lee, and dates from 1993. Most buttons are now elsewhere on the average browser screen and some labels refer to functions that are now automated.*

*(Left) A detail from a diagram by Tim Berners-Lee in 1989/90 showing the complex interrelationships that he was analyzing when designing the world wide web.*

# HOW DOES THE WEB WORK?

The world wide web is the fastest growing area of the internet. Because the web can be used to send and receive different forms of data to and from computers located anywhere, its organization and operation are highly complex.

### REQUESTING A SITE

The web works by a computer sending a request for a website to another computer (the *host* computer), which stores the website. The host computer finds the site and sends the site's data (text, images, sound, and video) to the computer from which the request originated.

Sender's ISP
*The Internet Service Provider acts as the gateway through which your request enters the internet*

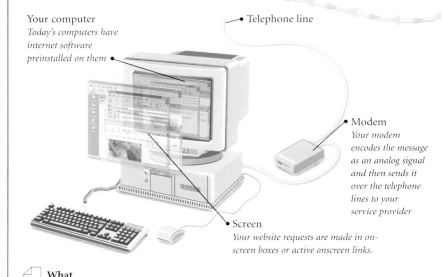

Your computer
*Today's computers have internet software preinstalled on them*

Telephone line

Modem
*Your modem encodes the message as an analog signal and then sends it over the telephone lines to your service provider*

Screen
*Your website requests are made in on-screen boxes or active onscreen links.*

10 What is an ISP?

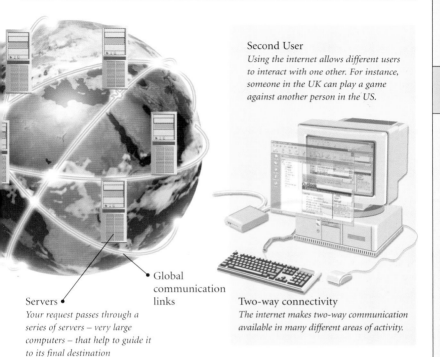

**Second User**
*Using the internet allows different users to interact with one other. For instance, someone in the UK can play a game against another person in the US.*

**Servers •**
*Your request passes through a series of servers – very large computers – that help to guide it to its final destination*

**Global communication links**

**Two-way connectivity**
*The internet makes two-way communication available in many different areas of activity.*

## ISN'T THE WEB THE SAME AS THE INTERNET?

Many people use the terms "world wide web" and "internet" to mean the same thing, but they are different. The internet is a global network of interconnected computers that communicate with each other via the existing telecommunications networks. The web uses the internet network to access and link websites. As well as providing the infrastructure across which the world wide web operates, the internet offers a variety of other forms of communications and resources, including email 🗋, newsgroups, and discussion groups. If the internet is like a system of roads linking places together, then requests for web pages, and the data from web pages, are only two of the many kinds of traffic that travel on this system of networks.

33 | **Rules for emails**

# USING THE WEB

To use the web, you need an account with an Internet Service Provider (ISP), a piece of software called a web browser, and almost certainly a means of searching the web, known as a search engine – all of which are explained here.

## WHAT IS AN ISP?

● The world wide web operates across the internet, and you need some form of gateway into the internet. The gateway role is offered by Internet Service Providers operating large computers, or servers, permanently connected to the internet using high-speed links. Your ISP is likely to use several servers for different purposes. If you are requesting or sending email, data is sent to the ISP's mail servers – one for incoming and one for outgoing mail.

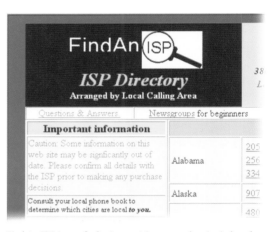

*Find An ISP (www.findanisp.com) is a comprehensive index of over 5000 ISPs in the US and Canada arranged alphabetically.*

## ISP OR ONLINE SERVICE?

Your choice of service provider used to be split between ISPs offering email and access to the internet, and online services (such as AOL and the Microsoft Network) offering well-organized and authoritative inform-ation, members-only email, and chat rooms. For example, AOL offers exclusive channels inclu-ding travel and sport. Recently, the differences between ISPs and online services has become less distinct. Many ISPs now offer attractive gateways to the internet. Apart from content variations, the main difference between online services and ISPs is cost. Online services generally charge a basic monthly rate to use the service for a fixed number of hours each month. Many ISPs now offer free and unlimited access.

## WHAT IS A WEB BROWSER?

● A web browser is a piece of software installed on your PC that lets you look at (or "browse") different websites. The most widely used web browsers are Netscape Navigator and Microsoft Internet Explorer.

● Navigator was the first to arrive and quickly became the most popular browser on the market. Microsoft then created its own browser, called Internet Explorer, and ever since, there has been a strong rivalry between the two. Both are excellent browsers.

● You can have both of them installed on your PC, and which one you use is a matter of personal preference.

### WHICH BROWSER?

The examples in this book use Internet Explorer, but the pages should look almost the same using Netscape Navigator. New versions of these browsers are released from time to time, and it is best to use the most recent release providing your PC has sufficient memory and speed to support it.

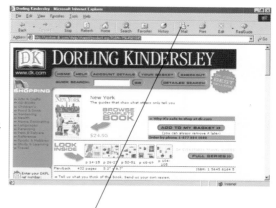

Internet Explorer ●
*Has a similar toolbar at the top of the screen to Netscape Navigator, but there are more toolbar buttons to carry out various actions.*

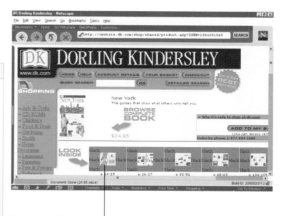

Netscape Navigator ●
*The pages look almost the same as Internet Explorer, but if you look at the bottom of the screen, you will see that the book pages are reproduced in a markedly different way.*

## WHAT IS A SEARCH ENGINE?

● To find your way through the possible two billion available web pages, it is best to let a search engine do the page finding for you.
● Search engines let you search either by entering keywords or by offering a directory structure. A keyword search lists sites in descending order of relevance. With a directory structure, you can "drill down" through the headings and subheadings until you find a list of websites that are related to what you are looking for.

● Search engines differ in many ways. Some are better at searching on the basis of keywords; others have more comprehensive directories. There are also search engines of search engines – these are known as "metasearch engines."

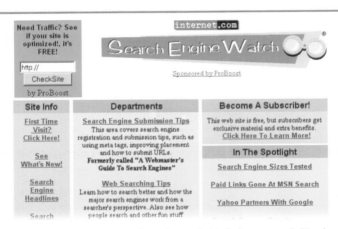

*The developer of www.searchenginewatch.com has a refreshingly direct approach: "People want to know what's out there, and they want to know more about the tools they use for searching."*

## SEARCH ENGINE CATEGORIES

| KEYWORD SEARCH ENGINES | DIRECTORY SEARCH ENGINES | METASEARCH ENGINES |
| --- | --- | --- |
| www.altavista.com | www.about.com | www.askjeeves.com |
| www.google.com | www.excite.com | www.dogpile.com |
| www.hotbot.com | www.looksmart.com | www.directhit.com |
| www.go.com | www.lycos.com | www.ixquick.com |
| www.nlsearch.com | www.snap.com | www.metacrawler.com |
| www.ussc.alltheweb.com | www.yahoo.com | www.webplaces.com |

## UNDERSTANDING WEB ADDRESSES

● Web addresses are known as URLs. This stands for Universal (sometimes Uniform) Resource Locator. URLs are made up of two distinct parts: a protocol and a domain name. The protocol part tells the web browser what type of site it is contacting.

The domain name, is the specific address, it tells the browser where to go to find the site.

*The familiar text cursor appears in the address bar*

## THE DIFFERENT PARTS OF A WEB ADDRESS

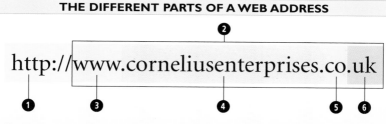

**①** Protocol
*Most web addresses begin with http://. This stands for Hypertext Transmission Protocol. This protocol is used to transfer ordinary web pages over the internet. Another protocol you are likely to encounter is ftp:// (File Transfer Protocol). This protocol is used on "secure" websites, for sending and receiving information that is regarded as sensitive.*

**②** Domain Name
*The domain name has several parts and is mapped to an Internet Protocol (IP) address.*

**③** www
*The vast majority of web addresses have www (standing for world wide web) as the first part of the domain name.*

**④** Host
*This part of the domain name is a name chosen by the owner of the website and can be, for example, a company name.*

**⑤** Type of site
*This part of the domain tells you what type of site the website is. For example, .co or .com stand for commercial sites; .gov for government organizations; .org for non-profit organizations; and .edu or .ac for educational sites.*

**⑥** Country
*Websites other than US sites also have a country code. UK denotes a website based in the United Kingdom.*

# What's on the Internet?

The internet as a whole offers electronic communication in the form of email, newsgroups, and chat rooms, while the pages of the world wide web can provide information on just about any subject you can imagine. Whether you want to know about astrophysics or Antarctica, golf or gophers, somewhere there will be a website devoted to that topic. Academic institutions have been joined on the web by charities and nonprofit organizations, public sector bodies, government departments, and, most noticeably, countless commercial companies.

## NONPROFIT ORGANIZATIONS

● Many major charities and nonprofit organizations have websites that provide information and opportunities to participate. Some raise money for a particular charity. There are also sites to anyone who, for example, has an illness and wants to know what forms of help, advice, and support are available.

*VolunteerMatch (**www.volunteermatch.org**) is dedicated to matching volunteers to different needs.*

## GOVERNMENTAL WEBSITES

● Whether you want to contact the president, your state representative, or the town council, there will be a website that can provide you with the right email address and a wide range of information.

*The website of the US Department of Education (**www.ed.gov**) contains a wealth of links and data.*

## ONLINE GAMES WEBSITES

● Many computer games now have multiplayer online capabilities, which allow access to servers where the game is being played. There are also free games sites to play board games such as chess, backgammon, and a wide selection of card games. Some web pages are owned by the producers of commercial games software and contain news, upgrades, competitions, and special offers.

*Heat.net (www.heat.net) offers online, multiplayer games, prizes, chat, web-based email, and instant messaging.*

## EDUCATIONAL WEBSITES

● Many leading universities and independent organizations have produced educational websites, which can include syllabuses, assignments, handouts, lectures, study notes, and examinations.

*Houghton Mifflin's Education Place (www.eduplace.com) is an educational website for parents, children, and teachers.*

## FANZINE WEBSITES

● Magazines for fans, or fanzines, began in print form in the 1920s and concentrated on science fiction. In the 1970s, punk music generated hundreds of fanzines, and by the end of the last century, the number of fanzines on the web exceeded 75,000.

*A British fanzine site (**www.smart.co.uk**) is dedicated to the work of Terry Gilliam – the film director forever linked to Monty Python.*

## SHOPPING WEBSITES

● Online retail sales in the US are now worth $30 billion a year, and retailers are doing all they can to increase their share of this market. One development is "reverse shopping" sites where customers state what they want and how much they will pay for it.

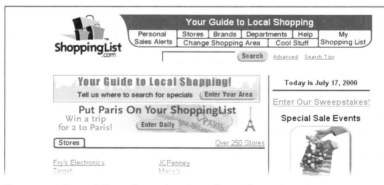

*There are countless specialist retailers on the web as well as retail megasites such as ShoppingList (**www.shoppinglist.com**).*

## GROUPS:
## NEWS AND CHAT

● Chat on the web is carried out in real time, that is, whatever you type in is seen almost immediately by everyone who is logged in.

● Newsgroups are similar to bulletin boards where messages are "posted" on special interest sites and can be read and responded to over a period of time.

*Liszt's Usenet Newsgroups Directory (www.liszt.com/news) is an extremely large directory of worldwide newsgroups.*

## FILES TO
## DOWNLOAD

● The internet is changing the way we choose to add new software. The internet is full of free books, music, videos, photographs, screen savers, and software, much of which you can download. Once you have located and selected a piece of software, the process of downloading usually begins by clicking a download button found on the web page, or by clicking a link that begins the download process for you.

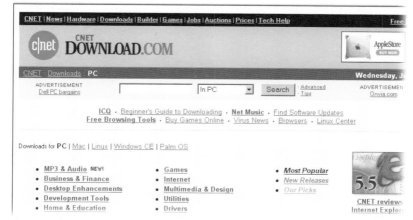

*Games, graphics, music, videos, and tools for your PC are all available from Cnet's Download.com site (www.download.com).*

# WHAT ARE THE RISKS?

**The value of the internet for information, education, and entertainment is undeniable, but for a young person there are dangers and pitfalls that parents should know about.**

## SEEING THE WHOLE PICTURE

Like most new inventions, the internet has had its fair share of bad press. In this chapter, we will focus on the downside of the internet, but it is important to bear in mind that, with care, the benefits of the internet far outweigh the dangers.

### BETTER THAN IT'S PAINTED

The popular image of the internet portrayed in the popular press as a force for anarchic evil is simply media sensationalism. There have been cases of abuse on the internet, but almost all resulted from either a lack of parental vigilance or from a child being confronted by a disturbing situation and not being able to discuss it with their parents. Neither reason is an argument for barring children from using the internet. That would be the equivalent of preventing them from entering higher education because they would be exposed to a greater number of vices.

*The 100 Top Kid Sites (**www.100topkidsites.com**) is only the tip of the iceberg as far as revealing the true availability of safe and enjoyable children's websites is concerned.*

## COMMON SENSE IN THE COMMUNITY

The internet is a community that is overwhelmingly helpful and informative. However, common sense is needed just as in any other community. You need to take precautions for your children's safety in the same way that you teach them never to hitch rides or accept candy from strangers.

Children can have their knowledge and experience greatly enhanced by being online, but they can also be targets for crime, exploitation, and undesirable influences. Children can be trusting, curious, and interested in making new friends. The worst response to these qualities is to suppress them. Instead, parental guidance, vigilance, and encouragement will help to ensure that your children's experience of the internet is a happy, healthy, and productive one.

# MAIN RISKS FOR CHILDREN ON THE WEB

Sex is most parents' biggest fear when it comes to children and the internet. However, other unsuitable materials may involve child molestation, drugs and tobacco, bombs and weaponry, gambling, hate speech, and cult/occult sites.

## PORNOGRAPHY AND THE WEB

● Pornography is big business online. It is estimated that there are up to seven million X-rated sites on the internet. It is expected to be worth $8 billion of the $18 billion that e-commerce will generate on the internet this year.

SafeNet from SafeNet Corp (**www.safenetcorp.com**) offers software with which web use is monitored rather than prevented.

## SEX AND THE WEB: HOW IT WORKS

From the invention of printing in Germany in the 15th century to the invention of photography and moving pictures in the 19th century, every new medium of communication has been used to depict sexual activity in various forms. The web is only the latest medium to follow this pattern. Accurate figures are impossible to obtain, but around 10 percent of adult material on the internet is free, while the rest is on paid-access sites.

Many of the free sites are bait sites that tempt people to enter, and then ask for money in return for more hardcore offerings. These sites use slang words for sex, which make them easy for children to access as they inquisitively trawl the net, in much the same way you may have looked up obscene words in the dictionary when you were young. The police are cracking down on some of the material but it is a far from easy task. This is where parents can play a role in helping to police the internet and to protect children.

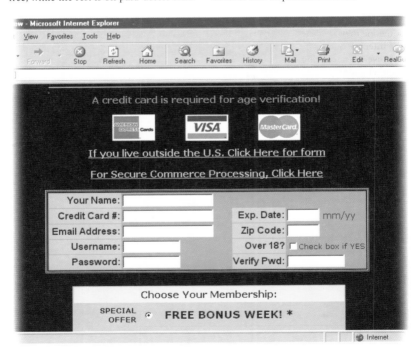

*One of the measures used by adult sites to prevent access by children is to ask for credit card details for age verification and an email address.*

## CHILD EXPLOITATION

● While surfing the internet, children may arrange to meet up with someone they have met online. Pedophiles have been known to use email, bulletin boards, and chat rooms to gain a child's confidence and then arrange a face-to-face meeting. Every month in the US, children run away from home to meet up with someone they have met on the internet. Sometimes that even means going to another country.

● Children may also come across email or chat/bulletin board messages with harassing content. They may also be harassed by companies in search of useful information.

*Exploited Child Unit*

# Internet Related Child Exploitation

The vast majority of information on the Internet is entertaining, informative, and educational. But the "Net" can have a dark s...

The growth of the Internet into a powerful, worldwide medium h... increased the danger to youths throughout the world and compl... law enforcement capabilities. It has simplified the method of exchanging child pornography, allowing an individual to receive... pornography instantly. In a matter of minutes a viewer can ac... download hundreds of photographs. It is not solely a matter of... pedophiles can use the Internet, with no precautions, to exchan... names and addresses of other pedophiles and of potential child... victims.

Background and Statistics

Tips for T...

Safety Guidelines for Children Online

Guidelines for Parents

Preven... and Reso...

Laws and Legislation

Background and Statistics | Safety Guidelines for Children Online | Guide... Parents | Tips for Teens | Laws and Legislation | Prevention and Resources | Child Unit

*There is a great deal of useful advice in the site of The National Center for Missing and Exploited Children (www.missingkids.com).*

## DRUGS AND TOBACCO

● The majority of sites on the web that are concerned with drugs and tobacco are devoted to prevention and treatment. Many sites contain advice for young people on how to avoid involvement in these activities. However, the first amendment ensures that sites can exist where certain aspects of these topics are discussed openly and in a less negative light.

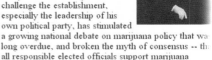

*Recreational U...*

Republican Governor Gary Johnson of New Mexico has recently spoken out about his belief that the war on drugs has been a failure, and he has proposed the legalization of marijuana. His willingness to challenge the establishment, especially the leadership of his own political party, has stimulated a growing national debate on marijuana policy that wa.. long overdue, and broken the myth of consensus -- th. all responsible elected officials support marijuana prohibition.

Interestingly, when Governor Johnson was first a candidate for governor, he publicly acknowledged that

*Norml's site (www.norml.org) discusses the drug-decriminalization views held by New Mexico's Republican governor, Gary Johnson.*

## BOMBS AND WEAPONRY

● This deliberately unidentified (but easily found) site contains details for making powerful and effective weapons of destruction. However, as the example below shows, the site is able, confusingly, to combine the truly macabre with the humorous.

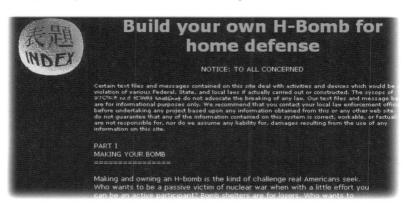

## ONLINE GAMBLING

● Internet gambling is a $1 billion business where national legislation has no international effect. In the absence of any effective laws, parental vigilance remains a necessity. However, gambling by minors is one of the most heavily monitored internet issues.

*Slotland.com (**www.slotland.com**) takes stringent steps to prevent access by minors.*

## HATE SPEECH

● There are countless hate sites on the web, which children may encounter. Some parents take the approach that, when the subject arises, it is an opportunity to reinforce the values that they would prefer their children to acquire and live by.

*HateWatch (**www.hatewatch.org**) monitors hatred world-wide.*

## CULT/OCCULT

● During the 20th century, religious groups have emerged that increase their membership through persuasion that may verge on coercion. Children are vulnerable to these groups, and so need protection and guidance in this area.

*This site (**www.americanreligion.org**) studies changes in beliefs.*

# REDUCING THE RISKS

**The potential problems for children surfing the internet can be reduced by parental attitudes, a commitment to responsible behavior by the child, and a sensible choice of software.**

## BETWEEN PARENT AND CHILD

Children, like adults, need some privacy, and parents have to respect that. But they also need handholding and supervising by parents in the real world – and the same is true in cyberspace. The most important safety feature that you can employ on the internet is common sense, allied with an informed, open approach.

### PARENTAL ATTITUDES

In addition to discovering the nature of the internet, talk to your children about their online activities. If your children tell you about an distressing encounter they have had with a website, it is far better to discuss it. When your children first get email, share an account with them so you can oversee what they are doing. Also, join your children when they are in private chat rooms, which will help the internet to be a rewarding experience.

### GUIDELINES FOR PARENTS

**Find out about the internet:** Your local library, community center, or school may offer free introductory materials. You can also use a search engine to look for websites that contain the text: *Beginner's guide to the internet.*
**Get involved:** Don't put up barriers between you and your child's internet experiences. Spending time online with your child will help your child to realize that the values you've taught them apply to the internet as well as your community.
**Keep it in perspective:** Overreacting to material that you find objectionable will either frighten your child, give them a negative reaction, or concentrate their curiosity, which they may attempt to satisfy.
**Learn the software:** Find out about the wide range of parental control and filtering tools that can help keep your child safe on the internet.

## PLACING THE PC

*Put the family PC in a general family place – the utility room or a spare bedroom, for example, where the children can be monitored. Don't let younger children surf alone – it is like leaving them home alone while you go out for the evening.*

## RULES FOR CHILDREN

Children can be given a sense of responsibility for their actions, as well as an understanding of some of the dangers of the web by agreeing to a set of rules:

**1** I will never give out personal details that would identify who I am, such as my name, address, phone number, school, or photographs.

**2** I will tell a parent or teacher if I see any bad language or pictures on the internet, or if anyone writes me anything I don't like.

**3** I will not reply to any messages or bulletin board items that are suggestive, obscene, aggressive, or distressing.

**4** I will not use bad language online, neither will I take part in arguments or fights online.

**5** I will not accept any offers of money or presents, even free offers.

**6** I will never order anything online or give out credit card details.

**7** I will not enter chat rooms and websites that I have agreed with my parents are off-limits.

**8** I will not arrange any face-to-face meetings with anyone I have met on the internet unless my parents consent, and they accompany me.

## TIME LIMITING

● Letting your children surf the internet whenever they want is clearly a mistake. The precise time-limiting guidelines that you set will depend on individual circumstances, but there are a few guidelines that can be used.

● The first might be to limit their online time to the periods when a parent is at home. A second guideline could be to strike an agreed balance between family time, homework time, and online time.

● Finally, a limit can be set on the amount of time your children are allowed to surf at random, because this kind of internet use will increase the likelihood of them encountering undesirable sites.

# BETWEEN WEBSITE AND CHILD

There is no substitute for the precautions and guidance provided by a parent, but a useful adjunct can be provided by the technology and software. Here we look at the options in sequence from websites, safe search engines, safe Internet Service Providers, and filtering software installed on the home PC.

## SAFE WEBSITES

Many sites can be found on the web that have been designed exclusively with children's internet needs in mind. They can contain information, games, and activities that are suitable for children. You can find some of these sites by searching for *safe kids' sites* in a metasearch engine.

New Hampshire KidsNet

## Kids Sites

<u>4Kids</u> – A fun, safe place for kids to be on the Internet.

<u>7-12 Kids Chat – for Pre-Teens and Children</u> – 7-12 Kids Chat – for Pre-Teens and Children

<u>A Kids Bee Hive</u> – A child safe site for kids of all ages. Featuring puzzles, games, music to do contests, and a message board just for kids. Lots of links to other kid's sites.

<u>A Toddler in a Grown Up World – Andre Jr. @ Home</u> – A toddler with a lot to get off his little Daily pictures and comments from Andre himself. Gain the perspective of one kids life, throug eyes.

<u>A+ sites for kids!</u> – Links for kids – individually reviewed for content, and suitable for all ages.

*New Hampshire Kidsnet (**www.mednexus.com/hp/kidsites.html**) is compiled by a group of New Hampshire pediatricians.*

**Search engine categories**

## SAFE SEARCH ENGINES

● There are a number of search engines available on the web that are designed to be used by children.

These search engines examine the websites that are returned by a search and reject those that contain any words that are considered to be unacceptable. Children are not prevented from entering any search terms they choose, but they will not be exposed to any undesirable material.

*Yahooligans (**www.yahooligans.com**) is one of the most well-known and comprehensive search engines for children. (Reproduced with permission of Yahoo! Inc. © 2000 by Yahoo! Inc.)*

## SAFE INTERNET SERVICE PROVIDERS

● There are Internet Service Providers that can provide web content, which has been filtered before it reaches your computer. ISPs offering this kind of child-oriented service filter material by using a combination of human researchers and specialist software to decide which sites are to be filtered.

# Squeaky-Clean.Net
## Family Friendly Internet Services

Squeaky-Clean.Net is a family-safe Internet Service Provider, offering a reliable and wholesome environment, specifically designed for children, students, adults, and business users...

Our mission is to provide a simple, easy to use dial-up form of Internet access that filters out objectionable material. Our Service never sends objectionable material to your computer !! We stop such information at its source !! In that fashion, your family employees do not need to be left exposed to the vast array of sites that support and provide information regarding pornography, drug use, hate, discrimination, violence and other similar negative uses of the internet.

Squeaky-Clean.Net is an access service. We do not, and will not, collect information about your browsing habits. We will not sell or share your e-mail address to others. Your privacy is assured.

We invite you to experience all the wonders that the Internet holds, without objectionable content. With Squeaky-Clean.Net providing your Internet Access...

*Squeaky-Clean.Net (**www.squeaky-clean.net**) is an ISP that scrutinizes all the material that it delivers for its acceptability.*

## FILTERING SOFTWARE

● The BAIR (Basic Artificial Intelligence Routine) Filtering System from Exotrope was developed to block pornographic pictures and text in web pages. It analyzes pages when a website is requested – before reaching your internet browser.

● An image recognition filter recognizes sexually explicit graphics regardless of the text surrounding it. A separate text filter evaluates text in context according to stringent criteria to eliminate the blocking of safe websites.

## HOW IT WORKS

● BAIR works in two ways. First, web pages are blocked if they are on a blacklist stored on Exotrope's central server. Second, BAIR constantly learns and adapts to the evolution of the internet. When BAIR encounters pages that are not blacklisted, the text and images are analyzed, and if pornographic text or images are found, those pages are removed before they reach your browser, and the page may be added to the blacklist.

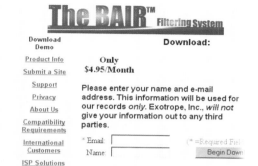

**The BAIR™** Filtering System

Download Demo
Product Info
Submit a Site
Support
Privacy
About Us
Compatibility Requirements
International Customers
ISP Solutions

**Download:**

Only
$4.95/Month

Please enter your name and e-mail address. This information will be used for our records *only*. Exotrope, Inc., *will not* give your information out to any third parties.

* Email: [          ]      (* =Required Field
Name: [          ]            Begin Down

If you have any questions or concerns with the install pr...
operation of The BAIR, please do not hesitate to call ou...
1-877-611-BAIR (2247) or e-mail help@exotrope.com

*Instructions for Dow...*
■ Click on the "Click to Begin Download" button. (Se...
■ If prompted, choose to "Run this program from its c...
■ If not prompted (some Netscape users), then down...
run it to install The BAIR Filtering System.

File Download

You have chosen to download a file fr...

bair321.exe from www.exotrope.com

What would you like to do with this file
○ Run this program from its current lo...
○ Save this program to disk

☑ Always ask before opening this ty...

OK        Cancel

Free tech support: 1-877-611-2247

Mor...
Info...

1-877-611-2247
Copyright © 1998-2000, Exotrope, Inc.

🗐 ou have any questions or comments about The BAIR Filtering System software download please call: 1...

*The Bair Filtering System (www.thebair.com) is available as a download on the basis of a 14-day free demo.*

# GOOD NETIQUETTE

Netiquette stands for network etiquette, and is a set of rules for behaving well online. We know that good behavior reduces the risks in the real world, and the same is true of the internet. Politeness and nonaggression are invaluable online tools. Surfing is a unique combination of being in the privacy of your own home while having a very public platform, and the dangers of forgetting this can be painful.

## COMMON ERRORS

● This unique situation can lead to three possible common errors:

● First, you can easily forget that people online are real. All you see are messages appearing onscreen – almost in the same way that inanimate software generates onscreen messages. People can sometimes overlook the vital difference between messages from software and messages from real people "out there."

● Second, some people appear to think that a lower standard of behavior is acceptable on the internet. This is sometimes a result of forgetting the difference between human and software communications.

● Third, and particularly when you're new to being online, you can make errors of judgment in what you say and how you interpret what others are saying.

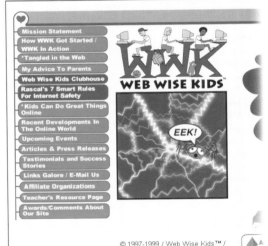

*Web Wise Kids (www.webwisekids.com) is an organization that commits itself to combining fun on the net with care for safety.*

● These misjudgments can easily lead to causing offense or to taking offense, which is when the problems can start. Remember that you are talking to people just like yourself, and try to imagine how you would feel if you were in the other person's position. Exercise patience when you see someone making a mistake. Sending a sharp message pointing out their lack of netiquette is often itself an example of poor netiquette.

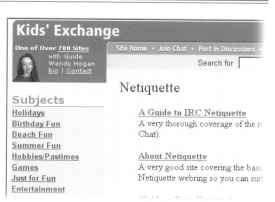

*Kids' Exchange (**http://kidexchange.about.com/kids/kidexchange**) is part of the About network and is an immense site for children.*

## MESSAGE CONTENT TO AVOID

● In addition to how you behave online, there are several content categories that you need to avoid or ignore.

● If you receive a chain letter, bin it immediately. Chain letters are always false, often threatening and alarming, and occasionally destructive.

## Netiquette Home Page

"Netiquette" is network etiquette, the do's and don'ts of online comm Netiquette covers both common courtesy online and the informal "ru road" of cyberspace. This page provides links to both summary and information about Netiquette for your browsing pleasure.

**"The Core Rules of Netiquette"**
Learn Netiquette basics by reading this concise overview network etiquette excerpted from the book *Netiquette* Shea. Shea's "Core Rules" are the classic introduction to and are widely cited in cyberspace.

**Complete Online Edition: Table of Contents**
Go deeper with the complete online edition of *Netiquet* Virginia Shea. This table of contents gives you access to such as Business Netiquette, The Art of Flaming, Egreg

*Netiquette home page (**www.albion.com/netiquette/index.html**) contains excerpts from "Netiquette" by Virginia Shea.*

## BAD NETIQUETTE

- Spamming is the practice of sending identical pieces of mail to a large number of addresses. Spamming is always irritating and can create numerous unproductive responses. Spamming is extremely poor netiquette.

- Flaming is the practice of sending emails that attack people personally, but is relatively common on the internet. If you are attacked in the real world, the best reaction is not to retaliate, and the same is true for the internet.

- Hoax virus alerts are too common on the internet. They usually contain dire warnings about nonexistent viruses, together with emphatic instructions about forwarding the email to everyone you know. These hoaxes can spread disinformation, they can be alarming, and they waste the time of everyone involved.

- Breaking the law is bad netiquette. Good netiquette demands that you resist any temptations to act illegally on the internet.

siblekids.net/

Parent Focus: Internet Safety for Children

**Responsible Kids Network**

*Empower Your Children to be More Responsible*
Internet "hotlinks" full of information to help parents teach children how to be more responsible and respectful of others!

*Parents' Survival Guide to the Internet*
"How to Survive the Internet With Your Kids" by Marty W. Stewart
Online tips parents can master in *ONE DAY*!
FREE! Family Internet Survival Guide!
(Order the book at amazon.com)

*Ask Marty!*
Submit your questions, get answers!
Frequently Asked Questions about Parenting and the Internet

*The Responsible Kids Network (**www.responsiblekids.net**) is more parent- than child-centered and contains a mountain of advice.*

you@321.net

MARY HOUTEN-KEMP'S

**EVERYTHING E-MAIL** ®

Sponsored by Mail Director, the best way to manage your e-mail.

### E-Mail Glossary

Common e-mail terminology.

*Everything E-Mail (**www.everythingemail.net**) is author Mary Houten Kemp's site that contains a wealth of email information.*

## RULES FOR EMAILS

- Don't set out to offend others with vengeful or hurtful emails.
- Don't write in capital letters, it will only be seen as aggressive shouting.
- Don't be superior if someone breaks a rule.
- Impatience is never a virtue. Wait for a reply to your question or comment before shooting off emails demanding a response.
- Don't overuse smilies and emoticons – the expressive faces made up of punctuation marks. They have their place, but it's a very small one.
- Before sending, read your email and ask yourself if you would say this to the person's face. If the answer is no, then rewrite the email with that in mind.
- It's very likely that your emails are stored in a place over which you have no control. Ask yourself if you would mind someone quoting your email back to you.
- The quality of your writing will be used to make assessments about you. Express your thoughts clearly, simply, and know what you are talking about. Use a spell checker – it will make your emails stand out from the rest.
- Finally, try to be a polite, pleasant, and thoughtful member of the online community. The internet itself is made a better place by each person who chooses to adopt these values in their behavior.

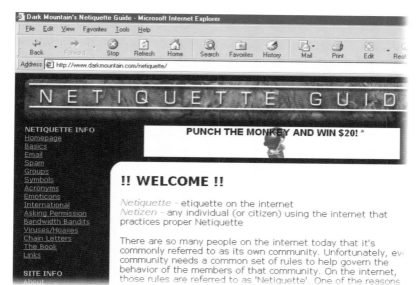

*This Netiquette Guide (**www.darkmountain.com/netiquette**) contains a broad overview of netiquette together with detailed discussions of netiquette-related topics.*

# SAFE INTERNET SERVICES

Only using safe websites may not give your children all the protection they need. The next link in the chain is selecting an ISP that can block sites for you, or to use server-side software.

## WHAT AN ISP DOES

You need an Internet Service Provider (ISP) to gain access to the world wide web. Your ISP will provide you with a local telephone number (called a Point of Presence, or POP), which gives you access to the internet. ISPs are not thin on the ground and many offer a connection to the net and unlimited free time online.

### FILTERING ISPS

● Possibly the most pronounced difference among ISPs is between those that allow uncontrolled access to the web and those that limit access only to sites that are considered acceptable. The limited-access ISPs filter websites before they can appear on your monitor.

Last Updated August 3, 2000

**Family-Based Filtered Internet Service Providers**

**Nationwide Internet Service**

*Note: This list is provided simply as an overview of family-based ISPs and does not represent an endorsement by Focus on the Family.*

| Service | Phone Number | Distinctions | Cost Per Month |
|---------|-------------|--------------|----------------|
| AAAIS.NET | (800) 575-9774 | National and international high-speed filtered access | $18.45 (other rates available) |
| | | Non-profit co-op has free and priority | $1.80 Membership fee |

*CitizenLink provides a list of filtered internet service providers at:*
*www.family.org/cforum/research/papers/a0002551.html*

# BLOCKING BY A SERVICE PROVIDER

The distinction between filtering and blocking ISPs is, at least, blurred. Both have the advantage of preventing unwanted websites appearing on your monitor by using software that cannot be tampered with by anyone in your home.

## INTEGRITY ONLINE

● Integrity Online offers internet access that filters objectionable material on the basis of human review. To find sites to review, a sophisticated research process is used that continuously combs the internet and identifies thousands of suspect sites every day. Using the results of the search, the review team then analyzes and catalogs each site.

● Once the review has taken place, access to inappropriate sites is blocked. In addition, searches by users that contain inappropriate words are also blocked.

● However, the internet is growing rapidly, and it is possible that a site may get through. Integrity Online ask that, if you find an objectionable site, you email them and the site will be added to their blocking filters.

## EXCLUDED BY INTEGRITY ONLINE

**Adults Only:** Strictly adult material.
**Hate/Discrimination:** Discrimination against people for what they are.
**Illegal:** Advocating or promoting illegal acts.
**Porn material:** Sexually stimulating material.
**Sex:** Sexual activity, merchandise, and fetishism.
**Violence:** Depictions of wanton violence or grave injury.
**Chat:** Sites that send messages in real time.

**Drugs:** Promoting any controlled substance.
**Tasteless/Gross:** Bodily functions and bad humor.
**Profanity:** Scurrilous language or gestures.
**Lingerie:** Models in underwear.
**Nudity:** Visible, sensitive body areas.
**Cheating pages:** Sites promoting plagiarism or cheating by students.
**Gambling:** Services relevant to gambling.
**Swimsuits:** Models in swimwear.

## COMMUNITY CHOICE

● Community Choice sets out to provide children with a safe and positive online experience through their expertise in internet content management. Community Choice uses a Direct Address Blocking (DAB) system that blocks inappropriate sites in the following categories: alcohol, anarchy, criminal skills, drugs, gambling, hate and discrimination, obscene/tasteless, and pornography.

● Their database of undesirable sites is updated daily. Each site that is added to the list is subjected to human review to ensure that it is not being incorrectly blocked. This method is claimed to be 99 percent effective, but as no solution is capable of achieving 100 percent protection, Community Choice includes an Internet Parenting Guide on every sign-up CD. This contains additional advice on protecting the child's online experience.

Address http://communitychoice.net/

Get *FAST*, **SAFE**, REL<br>
Internet access for your

### Main Menu

Join Today<br>
Access Numbers<br>
Cyber Parenting<br>
Filtering<br>
Affiliate$<br>
Home<br>
About Us

Community<br>
**Choice**.net

Child-Safe Access for Families o

Making the right Choice<br>
Service Provider can be c<br>
Finally, you can let your<br>
fascinating possibilities of<br>
none of the worry! Make t<br>
for your family! Sign up N

**This month's Cyberparenting**

#### KIDS ONLINE SAFETY

A great place to start for learning the basics of safet<br>
Includes tips and advice for new users from Cybera<br>
organizations on the Internet, plus links to other sit<br>
*http://www.cyberangels.org/childsafe.html*

#### WOW! KIDS DID THIS?

Interested in seeing some fantastic sites from some<br>
visit these award-winning sites, on topics ranging fr<br>
in between!<br>
*http://www.kidsdomain.com/kids/links/Wow_Kids_*

#### ARE WE THERE YET?

Do those trips in the car seem to get longer and lor<br>
ride and save your sanity? Learn several games to<br>
parents who have been there, too! Maybe the next t<br>
your kids!<br>
*http://familypc.zdnet.com/familycentral/travel/featur*

#### FUN SITES FOR KIDS-THE FROGGY PAGE

Interested in learning about frogs? This site has lots<br>
froggy facts. Everything from jokes and games to th<br>
of frogs!

*www.communitychoice.net*

# SERVER-SIDE FILTERING

Some companies offer a filtering service that sits between your computer and your ISP's servers. You keep your account with your ISP, but the filtering software detects unwanted content and prevents it from reaching your computer.

## ALLIANCE INTERNET

● This company provides a server-side filtering service designed to prevent pornography and material advocating illegal activities from reaching your home.

● Their filtering database is updated on a daily basis. The system is said to be about 96 percent effective.

● The blocking of sites is carried on the basis of content, not viewpoint.

*www.allianceinternet.com/*

## FAMILYCONNECT

● FamilyConnect uses a system called S4F, which is claimed to block over 96 percent of undesirable websites. S4F blocks specific sites as well as examining sequences of characters that are entered in the search fields of search engines. This will allow "Middlesex" to be searched for, but not "sex."

*http://www.familysafemedia.com/internet_filtering.html*

## NEHEMIAH FILTERED INTERNET SERVICE

● Nehemiah is a server-side filter that prevents the display of most material that is sexually explicit, graphically violent, promotes hate, or is illegal. Nehemiah controls access to web pages and chat rooms by filtering based on the address of the web page and a human review of questionable websites.

● With Nehemiah, the company alone decides what material will be filtered. You cannot choose what material you want to be filtered, neither can you permanently edit or override the company's filter list. The company does make available its criteria for filtering a web page.

● There are no password settings that might allow anyone to change the way the program runs.

● Your request to view a website is routed through the company's database and range of search filters. If the website is permitted, your browser is allowed to continue and display the site. If the site is restricted, your browser is interrupted and redirected to a "Filtered Notification Screen."

**Nehemiah Filtered Internet Service**

Address http://www.nfint.com/indexnew.html

In today's networked world, information on a variety of topics is available. Some of this information IS objectionable AND detrimental to office or home environments.

**NEHEMIAH Filtered Internet Service** helps you maintain a focused approach to business and a safe home environment for those that wish to be supplied with internet access that is pre-filtered and tamper-proof.

Keep and Dial-

No Nee

No Nee

Apply Our Filter to Any

*www.nfint.com*

## RATED-G ONLINE

● The content of the internet can be filtered either on the basis of included websites or excluded sites. Included filtering allows only those sites through the filters that are explicitly listed. Exclusion filtering prevents access to material that has been reviewed and judged to be unacceptable. Rated-G Online works on the basis of excluding undesirable websites.

● The list of excluded sites is compiled by using automated search techniques, evaluation by human reviewers, and constant monitoring of the web. The reviews are carried by a team of professional reviewers. Following the reviews, the company's databases are updated daily, and they now contain millions of internet pages.

● As with all server-side filtering, there is no software to buy, configure, or manage. Nor do you have to download new lists of blocked sites, which may only be updated monthly. Because the filters are located on a remote server, there is no software to customize, and the filters cannot be disabled.

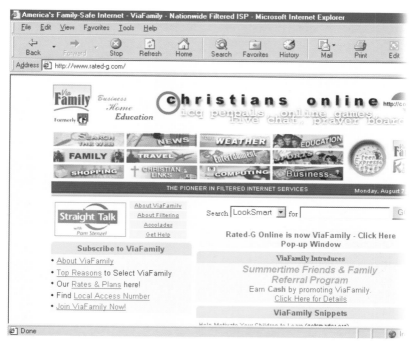

*www.rated-g.com*

# SAFE SEARCH ENGINES

Using search engines is an integral part of using the world wide web. The two kinds of engines suitable for children are the filtered mainstream engines and the child-dedicated engine.

## MAINSTREAM SEARCH ENGINES

To some users of the internet, the mainstream search engines are seen as the villains of the piece as their search results provide the addresses of undesirable sites. In response to this, some mainstream engines incorporate their own filters.

### ALTAVISTA'S FAMILY FILTER

● AltaVista's Family Filter (**www.altavista.com**) is a facility that can be turned on and off by a password holder and eliminates the majority of undesirable content from search results. The filter works in three stages. First, software is used to tag pages as objectionable if specific words and phrases are used in particular ways. Second, a filtering process traps material that the software search may have missed. Third, users can report pages that have slipped through the first two filters.

*Family Filter is currently off* ●

● Blocking is carried out on sites that contain references to drugs, alcohol or tobacco, gambling, hate speech, sexual explicitness, and violence. The filter also ensures that no internet chat rooms appear in any search results.

● The process is designed not to block pages that contain sexual terms used in a nonpornographic context. For example, a search for "breast cancer" should produce relevant results about the disease and treatment.

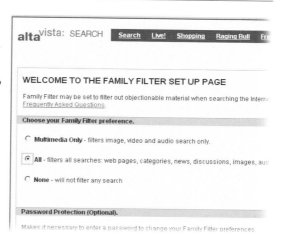

## HOW TO ENABLE IT

● Click on **Family Filter is off** to open the **Family Filter Set Up page**. Select either **Multimedia only** filtering or **All**. Enter an optional password and click on **Done**. Make a private note of the password, as it will be needed when you want to make any later changes to your Family Filter preferences.

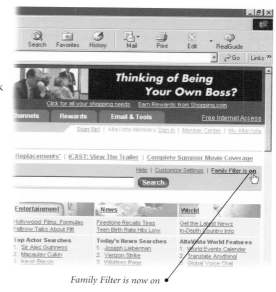

*Family Filter is now on* ●

## GOOGLE

● The search engine, Google (**www.google.com**), contains a feature known as SafeSearch, which screens search results for undesirable material. The technology that is used checks for keywords, phrases, and site addresses. The four categories of material searched for are: pornography, hate speech, drugs, and alcohol.

● The filtering information is kept as up-to-date as possible by automated website checking and by incorporating updates from Surfwatch which provides the technology. However, Google acknowledges that no filter can be 100 percent effective.

*Click here to access SafeSearch*

## HOW TO ENABLE IT

● Click on **Language, Display, & Filtering** option to open the **Search Preferences** page. Scroll down to **SafeSearch Filtering** and click the radio button next to **Use SafeSearch to filter my search results**. Finally, click on **Save Preferences and Return to Search** to close the **Search Preferences** page.

# CHILD-DEDICATED SEARCH ENGINES

Child-dedicated search engines are generally a very safe way of allowing children to surf the internet. In addition to the safe searching procedures, they often contain direct links to sites that are appropriate for children.

## ONEKEY

● OneKey (**www.onekey. com**) is a search engine that maintains one of the largest databases of safe sites for children. Sites are filtered out if they do not meet Network TV Standards. In addition, all sites listed in their database have been subjected to human review.

## SEARCHOPOLIS

● There are 30 different categories of objectionable material, including pornography and hate speech, which have been identified by Searchopolis (**www.searchopolis.com**) for exclusion from their search engine. Editors view websites for their content and they update the block list biweekly. Moreover, sites that are less than three days old are also excluded from search results so that editors have time to make a review.

# SAFE BROWSING

**Following the safe surfing features available in search engines, the browsers installed on your computer are the next level of protection that can be used to control the display of websites.**

## SAFE BROWSING IN INTERNET EXPLORER

You can prevent Internet Explorer from being used to view sites that contain undesirable material by using Explorer's Content Advisor features. These enable you to censor sites that feature obscene language, nudity, sex, and violence.

**OPENING CONTENT ADVISOR**
● Click on the **Start** button, select **Settings**, and choose **Control Panel**.

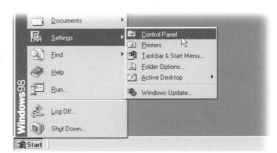

● In the **Control Panel** window, double-click on the **Internet Options** icon.

*The **Internet Options** icon* ●

● The **Internet Properties** dialog box opens with a number of tabs arranged along the top. Click on the **Content** tab.

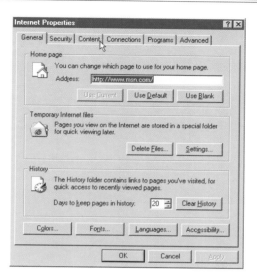

● In the **Content Advisor** section toward the top of the dialog box, click on **Enable**.

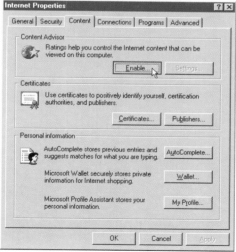

## SETTING
## THE LEVELS

● The **Content Advisor**
dialog box opens, and the
contents of the **Ratings** tab
should be displayed. Click
on this tab if it is not
displayed.

● The four categories:
**Language**, **Nudity**, **Sex**, and
**Violence** are displayed.
Click on one of the four,
and drag the slider below to
set the level of material that
the user is to be permitted
to view.

● As you move the slider,
the level number and the
classification both change.
A brief account of what the
classification allows is
shown in the **Description**
panel.

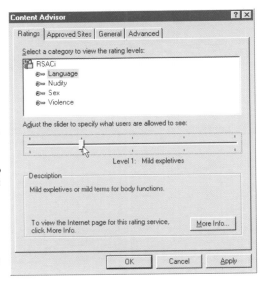

● The process of setting
access levels can be
repeated for another, or all,
of the categories. Each one
has its own set of
descriptions for the
different levels.

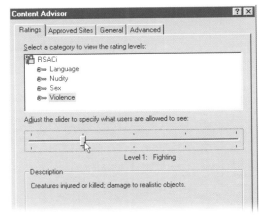

## CREATING A PASSWORD

● If you have not set up a password, you are prompted to create one.

● Type your password in both fields of the **Create Supervisor Password** dialog box. (Remember to make a private note of this somewhere.) Now click on **OK**.

● Your levels are now set up and only you, as the holder of the password, can alter the settings.

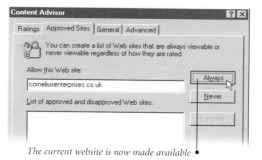

## ALLOWING AND DENYING WEBSITES

● It is possible either to allow or deny access to individual websites.

● Click on the **Approved Sites** tab. Type in the address of the website, and then click on either **Always** or **Never** depending on whether the site is to be allowed or denied.

*The current website is now made available* ●

● You can continue adding websites in either category. The allowed sites are indicated by a check mark in a green bullet, and the denied sites are marked by a No Entry bullet.

● Click on **OK** when you have finished listing the sites. You can add to the list at any time.

# KIDS' SURFING FROM NETSCAPE

If you use Netscape Navigator as your browser rather than Internet Explorer, you won't be able to find an equivalent to Explorer's Content Advisor. However, Netscape provides a browsing tool designed specifically for children.

### OPENING THE KIDS' BROWSER
● In Netscape's home page, click on **Kids** in the **Family** group under **Channels**.

*Access to Netscape's Kids' browser is available here*

### KIDZONE
● The KidZone page opens. It contains a number of links to a very wide range of websites that have been classified under various headings. Here, **Awesome Websites** is being selected in the center of the page.

## SURF THE WEB WITH MAMAMEDIA

● The kids' browser is provided by MaMa-Media.com, which is a company that specializes in combining technology and learning for children.

● The browser is opened simply by clicking on **Surf the Web**.

● The MaMaMedia browser has a directory structure reflecting the company's emphasis on developing word association and logic skills.

There are over 2000 handpicked sites that are constantly updated.

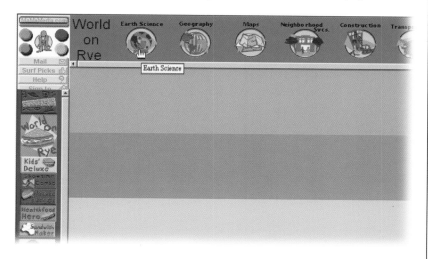

# RSACi / ICRA: The Internet Content Rating Association

Some web browsers that are either filtered or dedicated to children's interests make use of rating systems. One of the most respected rating systems has been created by the Internet Content Rating Association. This is a nonprofit organization that has developed an open, objective, content advisory system – the RSACi system. This system provides information about the level of sex, nudity, violence, and offensive language in software games and websites.

## EXPLORER AND CYBER PATROL

● The RSACi rating has been integrated into Netscape Navigator, Microsoft's browser, Internet Explorer, and Cyber Patrol software. In all, there are 160,000 websites that have their content rated with the RSACi ratings system.

● The aim of the RSACi rating is to provide a rating system for websites, which protects children and protects the rights of free speech on the world wide web.
● The ratings that are seen when using Explorer's Content Advisor are derived from the RSACi system.

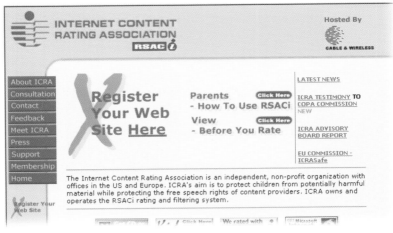

*Further information about the Internet Content Rating Association can be found on their website: www.icra.org.*

# PICS – Platform for Internet Content Selection

The Platform for Internet Content Selection is a technological standard that allows web browsers to read the rating labels of sites and, if necessary, block them on the basis of their rating. Website operators voluntarily submit their sites for rating by a third-party rating agency.

Once rated, PICS then provides a code that must be added to the HTML coding at the top of their site. While this code is not displayed onscreen, it is read by the browser and allows or denies access to the site, depending on the rating criteria set in your browser.

## EXPLORER AND NETSCAPE

Microsoft's Internet Explorer versions 3.0 and higher support PICS, and Netscape's next version of Navigator will include PICS capability as well. Not many sites are currently PICS-rated, although awareness of the system is steadily increasing.

**Platform for Internet Content Selection (PICS)**

The **PICS**™ specification enables labels (metadata) to be associated with Internet content. It was originally designed to help parents and teachers control what children access on the Internet, but it also facilitates other uses for labels, including code signing and privacy. The PICS platform is one on which other rating services and filtering software have been built. Parents who are interested in finding filtering software or ISPs that offer filtering will probably want to consult www.netparents.org rather than this site.

### Table of Contents

*The Platform for Internet Content Selection can be found at www.w3.org/PICS.*

# SOFTWARE ON YOUR PC

**"Safe computing software," or "smut busters," fall into several categories. They either block undesirable sites or only allow children access to what their parents decide is acceptable.**

## HOW THE SOFTWARE WORKS

Most of the safe computing software on the market today filter by using key words and phrases. Some go as far as filtering them in context to prevent blocking out innocent phrases. Some create onscreen alerts, so parents know when their children are trying to access unacceptable sites. Others block access "transparently," which means that when you are accessing the internet you are not aware that they are at work. This is the technique that is generally used in schools.

### BLOCKING
Blocking software basically does what it says – blocks out unacceptable websites. The methods used vary from checking a list of objectionable keywords, analyzing a site's content with software, to compiling lists of sites manually. Blocking lists are updated regularly by the companies.

*We-Blocker (**www.we-blocker.com**) is fully customizable blocking software. It is also free.*

## MONITORING

● Monitoring packages record the website visits in an activity log that can be examined by the parent. The log also records how long the internet has been used and at what times. These programs may also shut down the computer after a predetermined period has elapsed to limit computer use.

### Worried about your child's safety on the Internet?

The Internet opens the door to a world of possibilities...

*ChatMinder (**www.chatminder.com**) is a monitoring program.*

## INCOMING SCREENING

● This feature screens all incoming information to your computer, including emails. These can be from unsavory people children have met in chat rooms, or companies trying to sell them something or asking for personal information. Emails can also include links that can take children directly to adult sites.

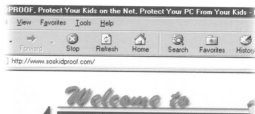

*Complete Protection for your Kids and your PC*

With every KidProof purchase receive a FREE Interne (retail value $13.00)
For more details simply call 1-800-427-9422 or contact
Click here for more information

## OUTGOING SCREENING

● Children can be fooled into giving away personal details on the promise of free gifts and games. Outgoing screening prevents your children from sending an address, telephone number, or credit card details.

Kids Will Be Kids... Whether they're
kids have a talent for getting into everythin
like hanging a big "WELCOME" sign out
right in and you might not like who shows
And if they have free-run of your PC, you
years of Quicken files have been replaced
You've childproofed your home—doesn't it

■ KIDPROOF HOME
■ FEATURES
■ EVALUATION DOWNLOAD

*SOS KidProof (**www.soskidproof.com**) includes screening features.*

# SAFE SOFTWARE PACKAGES

In the context of parental control, safe software packages are usually the first line of defense that is considered. There is a very wide range of products on the market, each with their own combination of features and levels of effectiveness.

### CYBERSITTER

● CYBERsitter filters material based on a filter file and scans web pages for unacceptable words. Filter files are updated automatically through an autodownload feature. CYBERsitter blocks pornography, drug references, hate speech, and newsgroups.

● You cannot set levels for different people using the family PC. You can, however, opt to filter chat and email, create an activity log, and set your own forbidden URLs. CYBERsitter is protected by the use of a password, which parents can override.

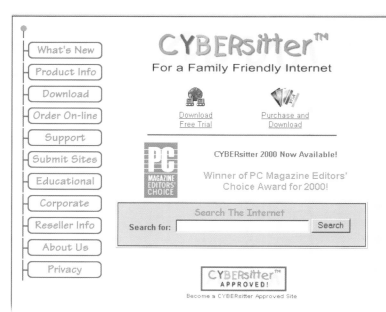

*CYBERsitter: www.cybersitter.com*

## CYBER SENTINEL

● Cyber Sentinel works in two modes: active mode and stealth mode.

● Active mode controls when the web can be surfed and which sites are accessible based on filter libraries, which you can add to. If the rules are broken, the user is warned, the violation logged, the program closed, and even the details emailed to a given address.

● Stealth mode surveys and records illicit computer use, which parents can review.

Sentinel is the most advanced
t filtering software package available
As parents and administrators, we
be present to continuously monitor a
computer activity. The software was
ed with this in mind and it provides a
proactive model for analyzing,
ng, filtering, and blocking
rable, predatory, and sexually explicit
er traffic. It is the **only** application

**Features:**

● Next generation internet security
  architecture
● Real Time monitoring in chat room
  mail, search engines, browsers, ir
  messaging, and all Windows®
  applications
● Stealth (invisible) or active modes

*Cyber Sentinel:* **www.securitysoft.com/cyber-page.htm**

## CYBER SNOOP

● Cyber Snoop is monitoring software that lets you know what and when has been visited on the internet.

● Log activity can be customized and any unknown sites easily displayed. The software also monitors chat and email. The keywords and site addresses for the filtering function take time to input. However, there is a start-kit list of sites that Cyber Snoop considers inappropriate for children that can be used.

Contents
Products
Cyber Snoop
  @Home
  @Work
  @School
  Starter List
  TakeMeHome
  Private-I
Purchase Products
  By Phone
  On Line
  Downloads
  Software

Cyber Snoop@Home

Cyber Snoop Internet Monitoring and Control S
developed with the philosophy that while we tru
have a means to supervise and guide them.

It is generally agreed, that we would like to kee

*Cyber Snoop:* **www.pearlsw.com/products/CyberSnoop@Home.htm**

## NET NANNY

● Net Nanny is capable of blocking almost all types of inappropriate material by using a list of words, URLs, and phrases that you might find objectionable. All online activity can be monitored through Net Nanny, including internet utilities, web browsers, newsgroups, chat rooms, and email. The lists are fully customizable and can be updated with downloads from Net Nanny's website.

● Net Nanny has filtering options, which include blocking the transmission of personal information. Parents choose the required action if a violation occurs. A violation could simply be logged in an audit trail, a warning shown onscreen, the words or phrases masked, or the computer shut down. These actions are all customizable.

● For younger children, you can create a **Can Go** list that enables children only to enter sites that you have found suitable. Net Nanny can support up to 12 user accounts and passwords, which means you can open up different access rules for each family member. All activities on Net Nanny are password protected.

*Net Nanny:* **www.netnanny.com**

## WINGUARDIAN

● WinGuardian runs completely hidden on the system and logs all websites visited and all programs that have been run. You can also program WinGuardian to tell you exactly how much time someone is spending online. Emails and specified email addresses can be logged. Win-Guardian can even log all keystrokes typed in and take screen shots at predefined intervals. Parents can review the log and detect if anyone has been running inappro-priate programs, such as games, or visiting offensive websites.

● If you have young children, WinGuardian is a useful security tool in that you can secure Windows so that users cannot run unauthorized programs or modify Windows configurations such as printer settings or wall-paper. This ensures that children do not tamper with your PC.

● This monitoring package is used by employers, schools, and libraries, as well as parents. It is fully password and encryption protected.

*"I was really impressed, a great piece of software! Well done!"* - 5 S
James Webb, 5 Star Shareware Reviewer

Click here to view a few full size screenshots of WinGuardian

Click here to read a user's testimonial for WinGuardian

### Details and Features of WinGuardian

- Logs user visited web sites.
- Logs all programs opened and closed.
- Captures all keystrokes typed into Windows programs.
- Takes screenshot images at specified times.
- Optionally displays an ACCEPTABLE USE POLICY on scree
- Can automatically email out log files for remote viewing.

*WinGuardian: www.webroot.com/chap1.htm*

## SURFWATCH

● SurfWatch is not as customizable as some of the other safe computing options available, but it is nonetheless effective and easy to use.

● SurfWatch checks for objectionable material in five general categories: sexually explicit, drugs and alcohol, gambling, violence, and hate speech. Categories can be switched on or off, depending on how liberal a view parents want to take. Sites that contain words matching SurfWatch's filters for each category are automatically blocked, and a **Blocked by SurfWatch** dialog box is displayed.

● SurfWatch is also able to block access to unsuitable newsgroups and can bar access to internet chat rooms. You cannot, however, set up multiple user profiles or block newsgroups without blocking the web, which might make it too inflexible for some families.

*SurfWatch: www1.surfwatch.com*

## GUARDONE

● Different analytical methods are used by different pieces of blocking software, and GuardOne uses rules-based technology to analyze websites. When a website has been requested, either by typing in the address or as the result of a search, GuardOne's technology examines the content of the site by performing a series of tests to determine whether it should be displayed.

● The technology used by GuardOne first takes the content of the site – the text, images, animation, links, video, and the programming code behind it – and digitizes it. The software then runs the content through mathematical algorithms to compare it against sets of rules to determine whether it falls into one of its blocking categories.

● In addition to examining the precise language and pictures that are used, the rules also cover how the text and images are related to one another on the page for a more complete assessment of the category of the site. This operation is carried out in real time and should therefore be able to block very new sites.

*GuardOne: www.guardone.com*

# CYBER PATROL

The exploration of the different types of available parental control contained in this book ends with a detailed look at one of the most popular pieces of software in this field.

## THE LEARNING COMPANY CYBER PATROL

At first glance, the wide range of options to exercise control that Cyber Patrol offers can be a little off-putting, especially for internet beginners. Cyber Patrol takes time to set up and requires a weekly download of data to work effectively. However, don't be put off – Cyber Patrol is a very highly effective piece of parental control software. If you are willing to invest a little patience and learning time, you will be securing access to the internet for your children that you can trust.

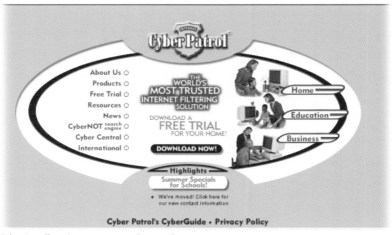

*Cyber Patrol's main screen: www.cyberpatrol.com*

# INSTALLING CYBER PATROL

Cyber Patrol's main screen contains links to other pages containing information about the software. It also includes an offer to download the software for a free trial period. Clicking on this offer is the easiest way to obtain Cyber Patrol.

## STARTING THE INSTALLATION

● Once you have clicked on the download offer on Cyber Patrol's main screen, the **Cyber Patrol Installation** dialog box opens.

● The first of several steps to start the installation is to click on **Next** in the dialog box.

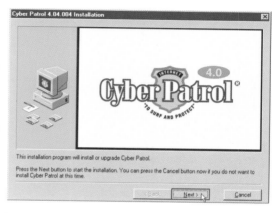

● There are a few screens during the installation process where choices have to be made. One of the most important is to decide what level of security you wish to install. The high security option is recommended because security levels can be adjusted within the program.

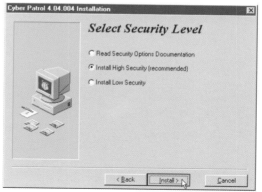

**FINISHING THE INSTALLATION**

● Once the **Installation Completed** screen has been reached, simply click on **Finish**.

# CONFIGURING CYBER PATROL

Cyber Patrol launches automatically once the installation process has been finished. Cyber Patrol now needs to be configured, and the first task is to set the passwords, because Cyber Patrol is installed without any preset passwords. These are important as they allow the principal user access to Cyber Patrol's settings.

**1 SETTING PASSWORDS**

● The first box that you should see is the **Cyber Patrol Access Checkpoint** dialog box. If this box does not appear, left-click on the Cyber Patrol button on the taskbar.

● Because there is no password to enter, simply click on the **Validate Password** button.

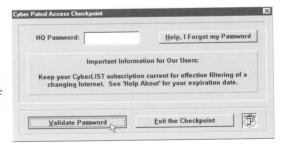

## CYBER PATROL'S HEADQUARTERS

● The first dialog box to open is known as Headquarters, where all configuration settings are carried out, and it is a screen that will become very familiar as you use Cyber Patrol's features. It may appear daunting, but it is very easy to use.

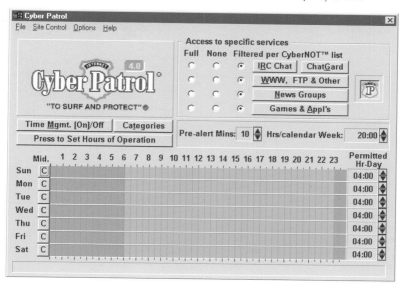

## SET HQ AND DEPUTY PASSWORDS

● Click on File in the menu bar and select Set HQ & Deputy Password.

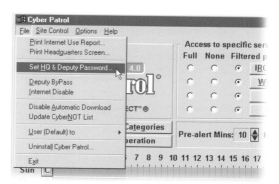

The **Cyber Patrol Passwords** dialog box opens. There are two passwords that can be entered. The first is for the person who will have access to Headquarters, the second is for someone who needs unrestricted access to the internet.

Click on **OK** when these details have been entered.

Cyber Patrol depends on Security. Ensure that only those in authority are present when you enter these values and that you remember the HQ password. Without it, you will need to call Support for Service!

The Deputy password should only be given to persons needing unrestricted access to the Internet. The Deputy can Bypass or Disable Internet access.

Normal-Disable-Bypass-Update

## 2 ADDING A NEW USER

Cyber Patrol supports up to nine users, each with different passwords and their own levels of access.

Click on **File** in the menu bar and select **User (Default) to**. Select **Configure User(s)** from the submenu.

The **Configure User** dialog box opens. Enter the name of a designated user in the **Users** text box and press Enter.

The new name is added to the users list. Enter a password if required, and when finished, click on **Save Changes**.

### 3 LOGGING ON A NEW USER

● When accessing the internet, the **Checkpoint** dialog box opens.

● Type in the users name, enter a password if there is one, and click on **Validate Password**.

### 4 CHANGING THE USER

● Double-click on the Cyber Patrol taskbar button, select **Change User**, and select the name of the new user. The **Checkpoint** details are then completed.

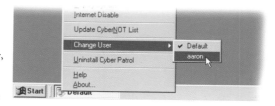

### 5 TESTING THE INSTALLATION

● At any time while you are using Cyber Patrol, it is possible to test that the installation is working. Log onto the internet and type **www.cyberpatrol.com/TEST** in the address bar.

● If the installation is working correctly, the **Cyber Patrol CyberLIST Checkpoint!** intercept message appears.

# CyberLIST Checkpoint !

Code:2

## 6 CLOSING FOR THE FIRST TIME

● To close Cyber Patrol after the first session, double-click on the Cyber Patrol taskbar button and select **Close** from the pop-up menu.

● The **Checkpoint** dialog box opens. Enter the **HQ Password** to confirm that you have the authority to close Cyber Patrol. Then click on **Validate Password**.

**Cyber Patrol Access Checkpoint**

HQ Password: _____    **Help, I Forgot my P**

**Important Information for Our Users:**

Keep your CyberLIST subscription current for effective filter changing Internet. See 'Help About' for your expiration

**Validate Password**        **Exit the Checkpoint**

# SETTING ACCESS LIMITS

Cyber Patrol contains many features that allow access schedules to be drawn up. These control access to different parts of the internet, and control when and for how long the computer can be used. The following examples show how it can work.

## BLOCKING ACCESS TO A WEBSITE

● It is possible to add any sites you wish to Cyber Patrol's blocked sites. If you want to make the site available again, begin by clicking on the **WWW, FTP & Other** button.

● The **WWW,FTP & Other Site Control** dialog box opens. Here you can add entries to what are known as the **CyberNOT** and **CyberYES** lists. Enter the site name under **Additional Restrictions** and click the **Save Changes** button.

---

**WWW, FTP & Other Site Control for: aaron**                                    ✕

Cyber Patrol restricts access to material on the Internet based on Site Controls, time settings, CyberLISTs, Category Restrictions, and these 2 lists. These lists take precedence over the CyberLIST restrictions.

**Additional Restrictions**                    **Additional Approvals**

www.all_xxx.com

www.cyberpatrol.com/test

☐ Apply IRC Keyword filters to URL Names

**CyberLIST Selection**
[ CyberNOT List ▼ ]   **LocalLISTS**

I choose to

[ **Save Changes** ]   [ **Delete highlighted item** ]   [ **Cancel** ]   [ **Help** ]   Ⓟ

---

## PROTECTING PERSONAL DETAILS

● Disclosure of personal details by children while on the internet can be prevented by first clicking on **ChatGard** in the Headquarters window.

Access to specific services for: aaron

| | Full | None | Filtered per CyberNOT™ list |
| --- | --- | --- | --- |
| | ○ | ○ | ⊙ **IRC Chat** / **ChatGard** |
| | ○ | ○ | ⊙ **WWW, FTP & Other** |
| | ○ | ○ | ⊙ **News Groups** |
| | ○ | ○ | ⊙ **Games & Appl's** |

egories

● The **Chat Filtering Control** dialog box opens. The box contains text fields in which personal details can be entered.
● Once the fields have been filled in, click on **Save Changes**.
● Cyber Patrol will now monitor online keyboard input and, if one of these sequences of letters is encountered, Cyber Patrol will replace it with unreadable blocking characters.

**ChatGard - Chat Filtering Control for: aaron**

Chat Groups can be one of the most dangerous areas of the Online experience. ChatGard is designed to watch words as they are typed or copied from the clipboard to "filter" certain words and strings of characters.

The famous Carlin-7 words are included at the front of the list. These cannot be viewed or removed.

**Specific Entries**

| | |
| --- | --- |
| First/Last Name: | roberts |
| Street Address: | 99 cooper street |
| Town: | seattle |
| Postcode/County: | wa 90011 |
| Phone #: | 8573 |
| School: | cedar hill |
| E-mail Address: | roberts@ |

Other words to filter:

Enter the information EXACTLY as you want ChatGard to filter it. For example: last name only or the last 4 digits of your phone number.

☐ Disable ChatGard

**I choose to**

| **Save Changes** | Delete highlighted item | **Cancel** | **Help** |

## SETTING TIME LIMITS ON COMPUTER USE

● The time limits that it is possible to set in Cyber Patrol can be used to limit the total number of hours each day and when the computer can be used. Begin by clicking on **Press to Set Hours of Operation**.

*Time limits are set with this button* ●

● The column headed
**Permitted Hr-Day** is used
to limit daily use for each
day. The total number of
hours can be set separately
for each day of the week by
adjusting the figure with
the spin buttons to the
right of the column.

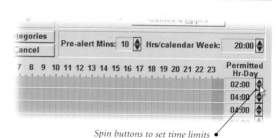

*Spin buttons to set time limits* ●

## RESTRICTING THE TIMES OF DAY

● The lines of red and
green cells next to each day
of the week indicate hours
in which computer use is
not allowed (red) and when
use is allowed (green).

● Clicking on the cells
changes them to the
alternative color. In the
example, computer use
before 9 A.M. on Sundays is
being prevented.

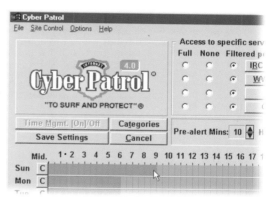

● Once the settings have
been made, click on **Save
Settings**. As with all the
access settings in Cyber
Patrol, they can be
amended as required by the
holder of the Headquarter's
password.

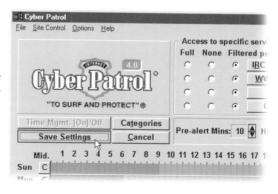

# GLOSSARY

**CHAT**
A conversation on the internet between two or more people, in real time, via the keyboard.

**DOWNLOAD**
Transferring data from one computer to another. Your browser downloads HTML code and graphics to display a page.

**EMAIL (ELECTRONIC MAIL)**
The system for sending electronic messages between computers.

**HOME PAGE**
The first page you see when you arrive at a website, typically containing a welcome message and hyperlinks to other pages.

**HYPERTEXT**
A term used to refer to the technique of linking pages together with hyperlinks.

**INTERNET**
The network of interconnected computers that communicate using the TCP/IP protocol.

**INTERNET SERVICE PROVIDER**
A business that provides a connection to the internet.

**MODEM (MODULATOR-DEMODULATOR)**
An electronic device that allows computers to communicate via a telephone line by converting signals between analog and binary forms.

**NETIQUETTE**
An unwritten code of conduct for the proper and polite usage of the internet.

**NETWORK**
A group of interconnected computers that can exchange information.

**NEWSGROUP**
A discussion group on the internet where people exchange comments and other information.

**OFFLINE**
Not connected to the internet.

**ONLINE**
Connected to the internet.

**PLUG-IN**
A program that adds features to a web browser so that it can handle file types containing e.g. 3D and multimedia elements.

**PROTOCOL**
A set of rules that two computers must follow when they communicate. Software on networked computers must be designed to use these rules.

**SEARCH ENGINE**
Software that searches for information on the internet based on your search criteria. Commonly applied to websites that host search facilities, such as www.yahoo.com.

**SERVER**
Any computer that allows users to connect to it and share information and resources held

on it. The term also refers to the software that makes the information available for downloading.

**SERVICE PROVIDER**
See Internet Service Provider.

**URL (UNIVERSAL RESOURCE LOCATOR)**
An address on the internet. You type a URL into your browser to visit a website.

**WEB BROWSER**
A program used for viewing and accessing information on the web. Microsoft Internet Explorer, and Netscape Navigator are the two most widely used web browsers.

**WEB PAGE**
A single page on a website that can contain text, images, sound, video, and other elements.

**WEB SERVER**
A computer with a high-speed connection to the internet that "serves up" web pages.

**WEBSITE**
A collection of web pages that are linked together in a "web."

**WORLD WIDE WEB (WWW, W3, THE WEB)**
The term used to refer to all the websites on the internet that are linked together to form a global "web" of information.

# INDEX

# ACKNOWLEDGMENTS

### PUBLISHER'S ACKNOWLEDGMENTS
Dorling Kindersley would like to thank the following:
Paul Mattock of APM, Brighton, for commissioned photography.
100 TopKidSites.com, albion.com, allianceinternet.com, aol.com, darkmountain.com,
everythingemail.net, exotrope.com, family.org, familysoftmedia.com, icra.org,
impactonline.org, MaMaMedia.com, missingkids.com, norml.org, onekey.com,
pearlsw.com, safenetcorp.com, securitysoft.com, slotland.com, smart.co.uk, squeaky-
clean.net, totse.com, we-blocker.com, webroot.com
Microsoft Corporation for permission to reproduce screens from within Microsoft®
Internet Explorer. Microsoft® is a registered trademark of Microsoft Corporation
in the United States and/or other countries.
Netscape Communicator software and website © 2000 Netscape
Communications Corporation. Screenshots used with permission.
YAHOO! and the YAHOO! logo are trademarks of Yahoo! Inc.